Women Over 50 Are Better Because...

Written by
**Jill A. Szynski &
Herb I. Kavet**
Illustrated by
Martin Riskin

©1997 by Boston America Corp.

30 29 28 27 26 25 24 23 22 21 20 19 18 17 16 15

Boston America Corp.
125 Walnut Street, Watertown, MA 02472 (617) 923-1111 FAX: (617) 923-8839

WOMEN OVER **50** ARE BETTER BECAUSE...

They can finally afford all the things they no longer want.

WOMEN OVER 50 ARE BETTER BECAUSE...

They can't be pressured into driving faster than they feel comfortable doing.

WOMEN OVER 50 ARE BETTER BECAUSE...

They know their exact alcohol limits.

They know how to start a car on fiercely cold mornings.

WOMEN OVER 50 ARE BETTER BECAUSE...

They start to hang around with new grandparents.
Of course, most are much older than they are.

WOMEN OVER 50 ARE BETTER BECAUSE...

They have achieved a reasonable accommodation
with their exercise program.

WOMEN OVER
50
ARE BETTER BECAUSE...

They start dressing for comfort rather than
blindly following the latest styles.

They are smart enough to hire someone to do the cleaning.

They can offer a critical analysis of every fad diet
to come along in the last 30 years.

WOMEN OVER 50 ARE BETTER BECAUSE...

They can shop for a car with the acuteness
of an automotive engineer.

WOMEN OVER 50 ARE BETTER BECAUSE...

They are never too scared to enjoy sex.

They don't catch colds very often
but hurt for a week after moving the refrigerator.

WOMEN OVER **50** ARE BETTER BECAUSE...

Their eyes are as good as ever,
it's just that their arms are growing shorter.

WOMEN OVER **50** ARE BETTER BECAUSE...

They actually look forward to dull evenings at home.

WOMEN OVER **50** ARE BETTER BECAUSE...

They know exactly which foods are incompatible
with their digestive systems.

WOMEN OVER 50 ARE BETTER BECAUSE...

They know the proper pronunciation
of at least three wines that they like
and don't give a hoot about which goes well with what foods.

WOMEN OVER 50 ARE BETTER BECAUSE

They no longer sleep soundly through the night but can fall asleep instantly at any dull meeting.

Their years of expertise enable them to know exactly
what is going wrong with their cars.
Still, they can't get anyone competent to fix it.

WOMEN OVER 50 ARE BETTER BECAUSE...

They've stopped smoking, drink with moderation, and eat sensibly. Still, they always carry antacid pills.

WOMEN OVER 50 ARE BETTER BECAUSE...

They have a few favorite secret recipes that can get them through any crisis.

WOMEN OVER 50 ARE BETTER BECAUSE...

They can afford an occasional splurge.

WOMEN OVER 50 ARE BETTER BECAUSE...

They can eat a double hot fudge sundae
and not worry about ''breaking out.''

WOMEN OVER 50 ARE BETTER BECAUSE...

They can smoothly put down propositions
from the drunkest chauvinist.

They know just what it takes to make their man feel good.

WOMEN OVER 50 ARE BETTER BECAUSE...

They have kids to help out with the real tough jobs.

WOMEN OVER 50 ARE BETTER BECAUSE...

They know how to organize a truly great party.

WOMEN OVER 50 ARE BETTER BECAUSE...

They don't care where their husbands go when they go out as long as they don't have to go with them.

WOMEN OVER **50** ARE BETTER BECAUSE...

They may have trouble with forgetting things
but they have their reminder systems down pat.

WOMEN
OVER
50
ARE BETTER
BECAUSE

They don't care if their man has a night out with the boys
while they stay home and sleep.

They don't nag- They have ways to gently remind people who annoy them.

They have great liquor cabinets.

WOMEN OVER
50
ARE BETTER BECAUSE...

They can ignore people who are glued to TV sports.

They don't pretend to be virgins.

WOMEN OVER
50
ARE BETTER
BECAUSE...

They are always appreciative of imaginative sex.

WOMEN OVER **50** ARE BETTER BECAUSE...

They can tune out even the worst snoring.

WOMEN OVER 50 ARE BETTER BECAUSE...

They have learned to live with pets.

WOMEN OVER
50
ARE BETTER
BECAUSE...

They don't expect as much foreplay
because they want to get to the heart of the matter.

WOMEN OVER 50 ARE BETTER BECAUSE...

They have a very low tolerance for inept lovers.

WOMEN OVER 50 ARE BETTER BECAUSE...

They won't blush at an X-rated movie.

WOMEN OVER **50** ARE BETTER BECAUSE...

They will be amused at romance in a parked car.

WOMEN OVER 50 ARE BETTER BECAUSE...

They are happy to hang out on the couch on Friday nights instead of going out.

WOMEN OVER **50** ARE BETTER BECAUSE...

They have more womanly figures.

WOMEN OVER 50 ARE BETTER BECAUSE...

They don't fall to pieces if you see them without their makeup.

WOMEN
OVER
50
ARE BETTER
BECAUSE...

They know how to handle temporary lapses in performance.

WOMEN OVER **50** ARE BETTER BECAUSE...

They have great lingerie collections.

WOMEN
OVER
50
ARE BETTER
BECAUSE...

They don't believe all the things men whisper in their ear. They don't get terribly embarrassed by them either.

WOMEN OVER 50 ARE BETTER BECAUSE...

They are perfectly comfortable with free thinking nuts.

WOMEN OVER 50 ARE BETTER BECAUSE...

They find themselves on virtually every junk mail list in the country. During the holiday season they receive 43 full color catalogs every day.

WOMEN OVER 50 ARE BETTER BECAUSE...

They've tried every diet known to womankind, but no longer throw out their oversized clothes at the end of a successful one.

WOMEN OVER 50 ARE BETTER BECAUSE...

They realize their father was right when he said it was just as easy to fall in love with a rich guy as a poor one.

WOMEN OVER 50 ARE BETTER BECAUSE...

They are willing to leave boring parties early.

WOMEN OVER 50 ARE BETTER BECAUSE...

Men at the office actually solicit their advice.

They know exactly what they like, and what they like costs a fortune.

They find obscene phone calls a mildy amusing
form of entertainment.

They don't believe all the ads for moisturizers and skin restorers
but they buy them anyway.

WOMEN OVER
50
ARE BETTER
BECAUSE...

They finally realize that no one cares anymore about what they did in high school.

WOMEN OVER 50 ARE BETTER BECAUSE...

They can remember the punch line to at least 3 dirty jokes.

WOMEN OVER 50 ARE BETTER BECAUSE...

They can single-handedly support the entire
sunscreen industry

WOMEN OVER 50 ARE BETTER BECAUSE...

They live in a place where noisy parties, littering, sex fiends, drug dealers and people crossing against the lights are all frowned upon.

WOMEN OVER 50 ARE BETTER BECAUSE...

They are no longer very concerned about being "with it".

WOMEN OVER 50 ARE BETTER BECAUSE...

Banks start to trust them.

WOMEN OVER **50** ARE BETTER BECAUSE...

You no longer have to give them birthday presents.
They plot revenge on people who
give them books like this one.

OTHER GREAT BOOKS BY BOSTON AMERICA

The fine cultivated stores carrying our books really get ticked if you buy direct from the publisher so, if you can, please patronize your local store and let them make a buck. If, however, the fools don't carry a particular title, you can order them from us for $8 postpaid. Credit cards accepted for orders of 3 or more books.

#2700 Rules For Sex On Your Wedding Night
All the rules from undressing the bride to ensuring the groom will respect her in the morning.

#2703 You Know You're A Golf Addict When...
You hustle your grandmother, watch golf videos and think you look good in golf clothes.

#2704 What Every Woman Can Learn From Her Cat
You'll learn that an unmade bed is fluffier and there's no problem that can't be helped by a nap among many others.

#2705 Adult Connect The Dots
If you can count to 100 and hold a pencil you can draw really sexy pictures of people doing "you know what".

#2706 Is There Sex After 50?
Everything from swapping for two-25-year olds to finding out it's not sexy tucking your T-shirt into your underpants.

#2707 Beer Is Better Than Women Because...
Beers don't change their minds once you take off their tops and don't expect an hour of foreplay.

#2708 You Know You're Over 30 When...
You start wearing underwear almost all of the time and no longer have to lie on your resume.

#2709 You Know You're Over 40 When...
You feel like the morning after and you can swear you haven't been anywhere and you start to look forward to dull evenings at home.

#2710 You Know You're Over 50 When...
Your arms aren't long enough to hold your reading material and you sit down to put on your underwear.

#2711 You Know You're Over The Hill When...
No one cares any more what you did in high school and you see your old cereal bowl in an antique shop.

#2712 Birthdays Happen
Your biological urges have dwindled to an occasional nudge and you discuss "regularity" at your birthday party.

#2713 Unspeakable Farts
These are the ones that were only whispered about in locker rooms like the "Hold Your Breath Fart" and "The Morning Fart".

#2714 101 Great Drinking Games
A remarkable collection of fun and creative drinking games including all the old favorites and many new ones you can barely imagine.

#2715 How To Have Sex On Your Birthday
Finding a partner, the birthday orgasm, birthday sex games and much more.

#2717 Women Over 40 Are Better Because...
They are smart enough to hire someone to do the cleaning and men at the office actually solicit their advice.

#2718 Women Over 50 Are Better Because...
They don't fall to pieces if you see them without their makeup and are no longer very concerned about being "with it".

#2719 Is There Sex After 40?
Great cartoons analyzing this important subject from sexy cardigans to the bulge that used to be in his trousers.

#2720 Plop
Let's just say this book is a favorite of teenage boys who find the toilet humor about the funniest thing they can imagine.

#2721 Cucumbers Are Better Than Men Because...
They won't make a pass at your friends, don't care if you shave your legs and stay hard for a week.

#2722 Better An Old Fart Than A Young Shithead
A great comparison of the Old Fart who dresses for comfort and the Young Shithead who is afraid of looking like a dork.

#2723 101 Outrageous Things To Do On Your Birthday
Wear a silly hat to work, jump up and down in an elevator, don't wear any underwear and drive straddling 2 lanes.

#2724 My Favorite Teacher
A super gift for a teacher that shows how to handle April Fools Day and outsmart kids who are smarter than the teacher.

#2725 My Favorite Nurse
A gift for nurses that explains how they make doctors look good, eject obnoxious visitors, and keep from getting sick.

#2726 Your New Baby
This is a manual that explains everything from unpacking your new baby to handling kids' plumbing and routine servicing.

#2727 Diddle Your Way To Success With Women
This book teaches how diddling works, basic techniques, first time diddling and how to know when to stop.

#2728 Sex After Retirement
Everyone needs a gift for retiring friends and this riotous cartoon book is perfect to help the retiree while away the hours.

#2729 Great Bachelor Parties
This book tells it all from finding a cooperative stripper to getting rid of the father-in-law to damage control with the bride to be.

#2730 Rules For Engaged Couples
Rules for living together, meeting the family, learning to share and planning the wedding.

#2731 The Bachelorette Party
Great pre-party and party ideas and suggestions for everything from limos to outfits to strippers to your behavior in bars.

#2732 Brides Guide To Sex And Marriage
Dealing with your husband's family and learning what he does in the bathroom and secrets of sleeping comfortably together.

#2403 The Good Bonking Guide
Bonking is a very useful British term for "you know what" and this book covers bonking in the dark, bonking all night long and more.

#2434 Sex And Marriage
Make your wife more exciting in bed and teach your husband about romance. Hobbies, religion and getting a husband to fix your car.

#2501 Cowards Guide To Body Piercing
Cartoons and explanations of all the good and horrible places you can put holes in yourself.

#1500 Fish Tank Video $15 postpaid
This fish tank video enables you to experience all the joys of beautiful, colorful and graceful tropical fish without having to care for them. You'll find yourself hypnotized by the delicate beauty of these fish. Approximately 1 hour running time.

BOSTON AMERICA C★O★R★P

125 Walnut Street, Watertown, MA 02472   (617) 923-1111   FAX: (617) 923-8839